MY
NEWPORT

A COLLECTION OF POEMS
ABOUT
NEWPORT BEACH, CALIFORNIA

SARA SALAM

Acknowledgements

I am grateful to the place I call my hometown for inspiring the content in these pages. And also to the people - family, friends, and strangers - I write about, without whom this collection would not exist.

Author portrait photographed by Christina Wehbe

Illustrations by Sara Salam

All rights reserved. No part of this book may be used or reproduced in any manner whatsoever without written permission, except in the case of brief quotations embodied in critical articles and reviews.

ISBN 978-1-7337263-3-7 (pbk.)

© 2020 Sara Salam
🌐 www.sarasalam.co
📷 @bysarasalam

For my fellow residents
who call
Newport their home

ALSO BY SARA SALAM

My Truth Journal

Love Isn't Linear:
A Collection of Poems About Modern Love

If Water Were Fire, A Novel

MY NEWPORT

A COLLECTION OF POEMS
ABOUT
NEWPORT BEACH, CALIFORNIA

SARA SALAM

The Peacock Pen Press
2020

CONTENTS

Introduction..1

Hometown Girl..3
Summer Love..4
Morning Walks..5
Fourth of July..6
Tide Pools..7
This Way..8
Twinkle, Twinkle..9
God's Seat...10
If Water Were Fire....................................11
JG Summer..12
Trident...13
Jetty & Me...14
The Visitor..15
Shimmer and Sway...................................16
Hippo Cookies..17
Crown of the Sea.....................................18
Someone Like Me....................................19
A Surfer's Prayer......................................20
Kobe..21
The Five Crowns......................................22
Bodysurfing Babies..................................23
Gratitudes..24

Thank You!..27
About The Author....................................29

INTRODUCTION

I came to Newport in the '80s.

I was born in the city's reputed hospital and have since called this town my home. I've seen this city evolve and change, and yet remain the comforting, coastal town that shaped me.

Most of my memories center around the beach, our backyard. With 8 miles of coastline, Newport is equal parts land and water – each about 25 square miles – a unique characteristic of our municipality.

The poems in this collection are a tribute to my youth, the formative years I spent here that laid the foundation for the adult life I'm creating.

You will find themes of water, like the ocean - fire, like the heat, earth - like the sand, and wind, like the breeze. Nature's elements commingle here, in my version of Paradise.

HOMETOWN GIRL

I grew up right here, on the west coast side
where the sands shift up to the shoreline.
I went to high school here,
got that Sea King Pride,
I used to cheer for our teams on game nights.

I've got an old soul, I still like to flirt,
I love who I love, I know what it's worth.
My spirit is wild and my heart is free,
You can find me on the 'ninsula, walking
      down the beach.

I can't hide my smile in the palm tree shade,
Can't help but slide 'cross the seaglass I
      made.
Boston called when I turned 22,
But I never forgot my hometown crew.

SUMMER LOVE

We used to dance and sing all day,
a couple kids making waves and catching
 rays.
cruising down the beach in your swanky
 Ford,
belting out tunes – "whatchu waiting
 fooorrrrr"?

You had your surfboard, I had my shades,
the setting sun closed out our days.
We chased hope like Obama preached
out here, holding hands, on the beach.

MORNING WALKS

I spend so much time,

in rhythm and rhyme

in moments of solitude that only exist as mine.

This time, I spend

traipsing the boardwalk until it ends,

breathing in and greeting the ocean air like an old friend.

As I pass my old school,

and chat with friends, old and new,

I think to myself, and smile, just like you.

FOURTH OF JULY

Summer daze
when the revelers come to play
amidst the local flavor that results in a craze.

The Fourth is a festive frenzy,
from parades, boat rides, and wagons 'o
    paddy,
patrolling the streets to ensure everyone's
    safety.

America's Birthday,
the red, white, and blue paves the way.
Water balloons and squirt guns on the
    boardwalk were banned,
Oh, those were good times we had.
I remember we'd chase each other to and
    from the sand.

Our traditions will continue.
This year, we will miss you.
This year, and all years forward, we will
    celebrate in honor of you.

TIDE POOLS

Anemones,
Trees
of seaweed
earthed into the chiseled ridges
sunken in
wrapped by rocks.

Barnacles,
swirls,
those oyster pearls,
hatched upon a shell,
where hermit crabs dwell
at home, in their tide pools.

THIS WAY

That California beach,
within Heaven's reach,
shores of sand beneath our wandering bare
      feet.

Your presence is so calming,
like bay breeze on Miami mornings,
the sonorous sound of two hearts –
      in harmony, they beat.

So when I'm deep, in sleep, where my dreams
paint pictures of you,
I see our memories play back in a catch-22.
When time stands still, and we kiss without
      shame -
I will always treasure us this way.

Kindreds sharing life,
exploring dark and light,
we laugh in bliss and take our pains in stride.
But all I really know,
You need space to heal and grow,
But I'm glad we both feel safe when we
      confide.

When you find my eyes, I smile in surprise,
I will always treasure us this way.

TWINKLE, TWINKLE

Twinkle, twinkle,
Shiny, bright lights.
How you glow and bring color to the night.

Decked upon halls and helms galore,
In patterns of Santas and snowflakes –
The crowds always want more.

Twinkle, twinkle,
Shiny, bright lights.
How you glow and bring color to the night.

GOD'S SEAT

God's Seat.
That's what you called it.
You said,
If heaven is Newport Beach,
This tower is God's Seat.
Nestled next to the sea,
a calm, subtle breeze
sweeps through the wooden beams
that anchor the lifeguard stand
to the grainy, white sand
that sticks to your hands
when they're wet with ocean water
and you climb up the ladder
to look at the view:
ahead of you – blue,
to the north and south – a shore wrapped in foam,
behind you, home –
the place where you'd grown
into the man we remember
as the hero of our hearts,
and though now we're apart,
we visit you at God's Seat.
That's what you called it.
You said,
If heaven is Newport Beach,
This tower is God's Seat.

IF WATER WERE FIRE

Clouds clutter coastlines
turning blue star fields into painted skies.
A sun eases down, toward our simple, sweet
    town,
and disappears as its audience scatters away,
    gone.

A sultry glow lingers, at the tip of my fingers,
a veritable vixen of light hangs on to the
    cloud's wings.
If water were fire, flames would idle in ire –
the day is gone, and the night is on fire.

JG SUMMER

Groms and gidgets,
Athletic yet (naturally) finless,
Take to the ocean to conquer it, fearless.
Wardrobed in red,
"Surf's up!" they said,
as they chased the horizon while waves
    broke over their heads.

Hard sand and soft sand,
JGs charge like a rock band,
strumming a beat that echoes through the
    sea and on the land.

Run, swim, run – swim, run, swim –
Who wins?
No matter.
This summer is the best summer there's ever
    been.

*JG stands for Junior Guards, shorthand for the City of Newport Beach Junior Lifeguard program.

TRIDENT

His crown of the sea,
Jewels of azul and seven shades of green.
A guardian, a god,
A perfect hero, hardly flawed,
Watch over the people who take residence
    on Goldenrod.

JETTY AND ME

I never slipped,
I don't think.
I just remember the rocks,
how slippery they were
after waves splashed on them.
I would run down the jetty,
tempting Nature.
I dare you to splash me
I would taunt the surf,
beckon it with my big words.
We sparred, in good fun, on the rocks.
And I never slipped,
I don't think.

THE VISITOR

Vacation mode.
Javier's at Crystal Cove.
Arcade games and ferris wheel rides at
Balboa Fun Zone.
Shopping at Fashion Island.
Duffy boat rides around Lido Isle, and
Bonfires and picnics and castles in the sand.
Good times abound
All over and around,
This beautiful haven I call my hometown.

SHIMMER AND SWAY

Shimmer and sway,
You shine bright today.

A metallic sheen of glitter and glow,
Your breath heaves gently in ebb and flow.

Howl and rage –
Your peaks engage –

Fighting furious under the sun's blister
Climaxed by a calm, sealed by a whisper.

HIPPO COOKIES

We used to walk our bikes down Marine,
towards Dad's where we stop for hippo
    cookies.
Storefronts change and turn over anew over
    time,
My favorite boutiques back then were The
    Persimmon Tree, Even Sisters, and
    Magasin 209.
But there are still fixtures today that remain
    as time goes,
Like The Village Inn, St. John Vianney Chapel,
    and Wilma's Patio.
A quaint cottage town linked by canals and
    gemstone-named streets,
accessible only by dock, by bridge, by the
    Balboa Ferry.
We used to take the ferry, on Sundays, to visit
    Marine.
Today, I still find my way to Dad's to get some
    hippo cookies.

CROWN OF THE SEA

Let me count the ways
I sing your praise
as I gaze over the cliffs of Newport's
      Back Bay.

You shine, you soar,
I love you to my core –
and yet, there doesn't seem to be a future
      anymore.

Like the crown of the sea,
you're still royalty to me,
my heart is so full and my soul is proud of me.

SOMEONE LIKE ME

You need someone like me,
Quiet yet free,
to love you like you always dreamed you
 could be.

I need someone like you,
Solemn and true,
to honor my soul and heal what's bruised.

We need each other,
as friends and lovers
to dream our big dreams and encourage one
 another.

Meet me here,
at the corner of Hope and Fear,
where we started our journey over two
 Helmsman beers.

A SURFER'S PRAYER

Waves bring joy to those who desire
a chance to surf a set of fire.
Surfing is a dance in which the wave leads
the surfer along his dance floor, the sea.

The sparkling, blue mass of water presents
a horizon in which hues paint dramatic
      sunsets.
The surfers look at this view as a guide
to their dreams that follow through to a
      heavenly ride.

KOBE

Shaken, stirred –
The moment I heard,
I thought, I hope this isn't true.
A presence so huge,
Transcending elders through youth.
A reality that permeates beyond this world,
It's not just about him,
Or his iconic grin,
Or his free throw backspin.
Life is fleeting,
And Death's greeting,
Comes whether we're ready or not.
One final thought:
Treasure your loved ones –
Daughters and sons,
In the end, we are all we have.

*While working on this collection, I watched a group of Mamba Sports Academy athletes working out on the beach, on a Sunday in early March 2020. Kobe's legacy lives.

THE FIVE CROWNS

Ye Olde Bell
inspired the vision, a place to dwell
intended for visitors, but became home,
to Tillie and family, who made it their own.
Today, Five Crowns remains,
A tribute to England in spades,
A titan of time,
A tenured wine captain's pour –
The Franks and the Van de Kamp's continued the story,
which is told today,
serving the best prime rib, patrons say,
A CdM gem – we're so grateful you stayed.

BODYSURFING BABIES

Jessie, Michael, and I
used to pretend we could ride
endless waves turned to barrels as salt
         burned our eyes.
Jess and Bro – more ocean savvy than me,
basically owned the sea
and took me along for rides – quite literally.

Fit and finned,
assessing water shaped by wind,
they glided for hours as if the session would
never end.
I made my own plan,
finding twirlies in the sand.
These days I miss, and would gladly relive
         again.

GRATITUDES

Yoga poses –
Long stemmed roses –
Henna tattoos shaped like a lotus.

Salty, sea air –
A rickety, woven lawn chair –
A boar's brush against my windy-blown hair.

Silent, blue dawns –
Fresh-cut green lawns –
The effortless waft of young palm tree fronds.

As I sit on this tower,
I'm a full-bloom sunflower –
I'm grateful for this life –
      minute by minute, hour by hour.

THANK YOU!

I am so appreciative of you taking the time to read this collection. Newport is very personal to me and I hope that sentiment came through in my words.

If you enjoyed *My Newport*, and would be willing to spare just two or three minutes...please share your review of the book on my website:

www.bysarasalam.com

Reviews help me get the book into as many hands as possible, and support my work as an author for the long-term (my dream!).

I'm grateful for your support and look forward to sharing more of my work with you!

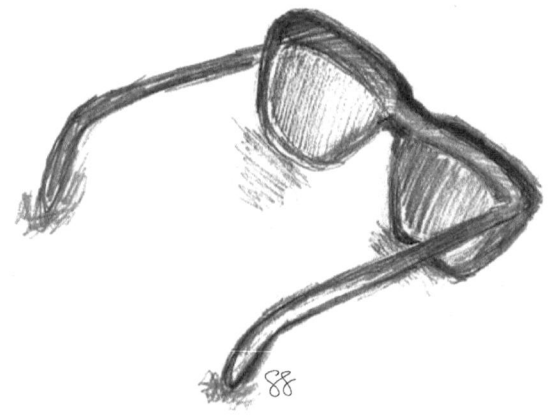

ABOUT THE AUTHOR

Sara Salam

Sara is an award-winning author and editor. Published since age 11, her writings range across fiction and nonfiction, poetry, movie reviews, newspaper and magazine articles, blog posts, and journals. Sara resides in Southern California where she enjoys writing, yoga and the beach.

www.ingramcontent.com/pod-product-compliance
Lightning Source LLC
Chambersburg PA
CBHW060508080526
44584CB00015B/1602